WHEN God SPEAKS

Tuning In to Our Talkative God

Harold Bonner

Beacon Hill Press of Kansas City
Kansas City, Missouri

Copyright 1999
by Beacon Hill Press of Kansas City

ISBN 083-411-8122

Printed in the
United States of America

Cover Design: Michael Walsh

Library of Congress Cataloging-in-Publication Data

Bonner, Harold.
    When God speaks : tuning in to our talkative God / Harold Bonner.
        p.   cm.
    ISBN 0-8341-1812-2 pb
    1. Paul, the Apostle, Saint.   2. Revelation—Biblical teaching.   3. Christian life—Biblical teaching.   4. Bible.   N.T.   Acts—Criticism, interpretation, etc.   I. Title.
    BS2506.B615   1999
    226.6'06—dc21   99-24252
                                                                                                              CIP

10   9   8   7   6   5   4   3   2   1

Contents

About the Author

Harold "Hal" Bonner is pastor emeritus and minister of pastoral care at Parkside Church of the Nazarene in Auburn, California, where he served as senior pastor for 24 years, from 1973 until his retirement in 1997. He is a graduate of Pasadena College (now Point Loma Nazarene University) and Nazarene Theological Seminary and served 44 years as pastor of a number of churches throughout California. A frequent contributor of Sunday School lessons and other articles, he is the author of *Second-String Heroes, First-Class Saints* and compiler and editor of the three-title series that includes *Proclaiming the Spirit, Proclaiming the Savior,* and *Proclaiming Good News on Special Days.* He and his wife, Gay, have three children and five grandchildren.

Preface

Not everyone believes in a God who speaks—but Christians strongly do.

We believe God has spoken eternally in His Son, our Lord Jesus Christ, the living Word of God, and in the Bible, the written Word of God.

The testimony of God's people is that God, in His own way and in His own time, comes with personal words—words revealing direction, imparting strength, and granting assurance.

Most of us wish that God would speak personally and powerfully to us more often. Most of us can recall only a handful of times when we were on holy ground, hearing the Creator-God speaking our names and revealing His message. The truth is that these moments, whether they are few or many, have shaped our lives. When God speaks—really speaks—we can never be the same.

The apostle Paul testifies to a number of conversations with God. In this short work we find insights from these conversations. We discover that God speaks to Paul when he is in difficult situations, when life was in crisis and help was desperately needed. What we also discover is that for Paul, every message from God is positive, not negative. In each hour of alarm, when God speaks, it is a word not of condemnation but of encouragement and assurance.

We discover that God's words to Paul are the same words He keeps on saying to His people—now—if we have spiritual ears to hear and surrendered wills to obey.

"I Want You"

Acts 9:1-20; 26:12-29

*S*ince the first discovery of God as one who speaks, humanity has been trying to put words into God's mouth; begging in His name for physical desires—claiming God's endorsement for human wishes.

And God does speak. The question is—*how* does He speak, and how can I know for certain that it's God's voice and not the voice of someone else?

The Christian community is confident that the God of creation and redemption communicates with His people in a number of ways. First, He speaks through His Word, the Bible.

Throughout the centuries, worshiping souls have heard God in the Scriptures—thundering in the Law, comforting in the Psalms, working in the history, evangelizing in the Gospels, and teaching in the Epistles. What Paul says to Timothy validates itself across the centuries: "All Scripture is God-breathed and is useful for teaching, rebuking, correcting and training in righteousness, so that the man of God may be thoroughly equipped for every good work" (2 Tim. 3:16-17).

And the hymn "How Firm a Foundation" reminds us, "What more can He say than to you He hath said, / To you who for refuge to Jesus have fled?"

Second, God also speaks through the collective wisdom of the Church, the Body of Christ, through its creeds and counsels. Paul warns against paying little attention to this voice of God when he asks the Corinthian church, "Do you despise the church of God . . . ?" (1 Cor. 11:22).

John Wesley places Christian tradition, or the wisdom of the Church, along with Scripture, reason, and experience as the resources of Christian belief and practice.

The third point is that God speaks through a Spirit-trained conscience. Who would steal when the sentinel of conscience is waving red flags of warning and shouting alarm of approaching moral violation? Paul testifies before Governor Felix and his court, "So I strive always to keep my conscience clear before God and man" (Acts 24:16).

Fourth, God speaks through open and closed doors. Such messages may be subtle or sensational, but they can be as much of God as of chance. The closed door of Asia, for whatever reason, becomes a holy prelude to the open door of Europe for the apostle Paul and his companions. As the writer of Acts concludes, "God had called us to preach the gospel to them" (Acts 16:10).

Fifth, God speaks through what we might label "sanctified human judgment"—the conclusions of human reason sincerely seeking the will of God. Such is the communication of God to and through the Early Church as they debate the crucial issue of Gentile admission to the Christian community. So, they agree, "It seemed good to the Holy Spirit and to us not to burden you with anything beyond the following requirements" (Acts 15:28).

God does not write this directive on tablets of stone or scribble it on the walls of their meeting rooms, but He accurately guides their sincere thinking.

And last, God speaks by direct revelation through the Holy Spirit. These are moments when we know that we have been in the immediate presence of God, standing on holy ground, hearing the divine voice and being gripped by the divine hand.

Paul has no doubt that what happened on the road outside Damascus is this kind of an encounter, one that has changed him forever (Acts 9:1-9).

For most of us, the communications of God come primarily through the first five avenues. It seems that for most Christians there are only a small handful of occasions when we come face-to-face with God. I for one wish it were more often—times when God splits the curtain of obscurity, thundering His word in my ear and whispering it crisply in my heart—"This is what I want. This is My will for you." But for reasons known only to God, it is often not so. One encounter with God is all we really need, though. The few times God has spoken my name have changed my life forever.

Paul testifies to several conversations with God, times when the Lord came and spoke clearly and convincingly to him. I believe his testimony is true. As I examine what Paul relates as God speaking to him, I have come to believe these are the very words God is saying to me—to us.

Our purpose in this modest study is to examine these conversations. As we do, we can't help but affirm that God has either said these things to us or that He is saying these very words now.

We begin with the first recorded conversation of God with Paul. What does He say in this first noted moment of spiritual revelation? He says in essence, *I want you!*

I. THE CRUCIAL MOMENT

This history is recorded in Acts 9:1-8. At this point in his life, Paul (then Saul) is an ambitious man in his middle 30s with a university-trained mind, a legalistic and explosive temperament, and a single, driving purpose to defend his Jewish heritage. He is committed to eliminating the spreading heresy of Christianity, which at the time is a five-year-old movement proclaiming Jesus of Nazareth as the Messiah of God—incarnate, crucified, risen, and coming again.

With official sanctions from the Jewish hierarchy, Saul had been an approving witness at the mob execution of Stephen (see Acts 22:20). He had been authorized by his religious leaders to take whatever steps were necessary to crush the emerging Christian faith and to harass its converts.

This is what brings Saul to the road outside the ancient city of Damascus. The year is approximately A.D. 35. Saul is on a manhunt for Christians. If he finds any, he has been given authority to take them prisoners and haul them away to Jerusalem for punishment (see Acts 9:2).

Then the incredible happens. It is about noon when Saul sees a blazing light that knocks him to the ground, and he hears a voice he cannot ignore.

"Saul, Saul, why do you persecute me?" (Acts 9:4).

Nothing like this has ever happened to Saul before. He ventures words he never imagined he would utter, "Who are you, Lord?"

And he hears words he really doesn't want to hear—words that would change his life forever—"I am Jesus, whom you are persecuting. . . . Now get up and go into the city, and you will be told what you must do" (Acts 9:5-6).

God's spoken word changes Saul's life forever.

It is a *powerful* moment. We call it a moment of conviction. We understand it as the work of God's Holy Spirit, whose ministry includes confronting us with our need and presenting us with God's grace through Jesus (John 16:8). The Holy Spirit comes to tell us that on our own we are lost; however, there's a way home. He informs us of the empty poverty of our seeming success and the one way out of our despair.

No one at the moment of overwhelming conviction enjoys this revelation. It is an agonizing travail, for the soul is torn from its comfort of life and lifestyle. In reality, it is the beginning of God's redeeming work, His only road to rescue, salvation, and life.

For Saul it is also a very *personal* moment. His companions see the light and hear sounds, but they don't understand what is happening (Acts 9:7; 22:9; 26:13).

God is very personal in this speaking to Saul, as He always is in speaking to each of us.

"Saul, Saul, why do you persecute me?"

This should not surprise us. Our God of the universe is incredibly personal. He has each of us on His heart. He never deals in nameless anonymity. As one writer observes, God does His business retail, not wholesale.

He had responded in the same personal way with Moses in the sacred hour on the back side of a barren desert, where a bush burned and was not consumed. The God of glory personally called out, "Moses, Moses!" (Exod. 3:4).

He was that way with a tender young man named Jeremiah, for God said, "Before you were born I set you apart" (Jer. 1:5). Every child of God *is* a child of God—because of a moment when God became personal and spoke his or her name and said, "I want you—come home now!"

After calling out a person's name, God speaks His message *precisely.* The word from God this particular day in Saul's life is not long, but it's long enough—clear and precise—to communicate His point. It's simple enough to lay the foundation for redeeming grace to do its work.

In essence, when God speaks, saying, "I want you," He is saying three things to Saul:

First He says, "Saul, you belong on God's side." "Why are you persecuting me?" (Acts 9:4). "Why are you doing this? Isn't it difficult to fight My way and to resist My will?"

Second, He says, "Saul, you belong to God's Son." "I am Jesus, whom you are persecuting" (v. 5). He is saying, "I am not a fictional character; I am no heresy. I am the Savior, crucified, risen, and coming again."

Third, God says, "You belong in God's service." "Get up and go into the city and you will be told what you must do" (v. 6). And he did, changed from Saul to Paul. And he was; on God's side, to God's Son, and in God's service.

Not every conversion is as spectacular or dramatic as the apostle Paul's. Not every call to ministry is as compressed into the conversion moment as was his. God deals with us individually, tailoring His touch according to our person and our needs.

Acts 16 records a wide range of conversion experience, from the youthful openness of Timothy, to the gentle but sincere birth of faith in the noble Lydia, to the radical transformation of the hardened and calloused Philippian jailer. God is as tender as possible but as harsh as necessary. With Paul He knew He had to be as blunt as a baseball bat.

Some people don't want God to talk to them, especially not in this direct way. Deep down inside they have decided they want no part of Him. This is evidence of humanity's fallen nature, rebelling and running from the God who made us for himself. These people are, as Francis Thompson put it in "The

Hound of Heaven," "fearing, lest having him, they have nothing else beside." Perhaps the hurry to avoid conversation with God is because of God's tendency to say the words He is always saying, "I want you. It is time to quit your nonsense. Come home to Me now!"

Those words of God are at the heart of every authentic conversion to Christ. It may be tender as with a child or exceedingly tough as with a prodigal far from home. But it is the penetration of the voice that will not be stilled that breaks at last the paralysis of the far country.

All conversions are glorious. Each in its own way is unique. But each in its own way is common as well, a yes to the call of God.

No record of Christian conversion has been more moving than that of Augustine. The passing of time (he was baptized on Easter Sunday, A.D. 387) has not diminished the timelessness of his spiritual journey from darkness to faith. The son of a pagan father, Patricius, and a Christian mother, Monica, he abandoned the faith of his mother in his teen years and embraced the immorality of the culture around him. At the age of 18 he took a mistress, who remained with him for about 13 years and bore him a son, Adeodatus. He joined the cults of his time and was trained in rhetoric. He went to Rome and began a school of his own. In 384 he was appointed professor of rhetoric in Milan.

At age 30 something was still very empty within Augustine. He tried to unleash himself from his immoral ways, but without success. He pleaded hesitatingly, "O God, grant me chastity and purity. But not yet."

The day came that would change Augustine's life forever. In the garden of a friend, as he struggled with his inner needs, he heard the singing of children at play: "Take up and read. Take up and read." Sensing it to be a directive from God, he opened a New Testament scroll and read what we now recognize as Rom. 13:13-14: "Not in orgies and drunkenness, not in sexual immorality and debauchery, not in dissension and jealousy. Rather, clothe yourselves with the Lord Jesus Christ, and do not think about how to gratify the desires of the sinful nature."

Augustine the seeker became Augustine the finder. God

used many keys to bring him home, including the prayers of his mother, Monica; the influence of Ambrose, the Bishop of Milan; the encouragement of Christian friends; and the self-destructiveness of sin. All those things came together in Augustine's surrender and his enduring confession, "Thou has made us for Thyself, O God, and our souls are restless till they rest in Thee." But at the heart of it all was the voice of God saying to him, "I want you."

That day on the road to Damascus, God spoke to Paul, and he came home to his God. In the miracle of grace, God began fashioning a new man in Christ Jesus. Paul would never be the same.

Do you long for God to speak to you? He already is! He is saying, "I want you."

II. THE CHANGELESS MESSAGE

Conversion moments are only the beginning. No matter how revolutionary or how quiet they may be, they are just the first page of the Christian life. The "get up" of the voice of God is always preface to the "go" of the voice of God.

So we "fast forward" to Acts 26. Some 26 years have elapsed. Paul is now in his 60s. Much has happened over those two-and-one-half decades. The first 7 to 10 years had been spent quietly and privately in Tarsus while God molded his life, softened his heart, and fine-tuned his theology. After that, Paul was on a fast track for his Savior. Summoned by his old benefactor, Barnabas, to assist in the ministry in Antioch (see Acts 11), he had been commissioned to pioneer a gospel road of Christian missions throughout the Mediterranean world. There were great episodes of power and glory in addition to devastating moments of persecution and abuse.

In Acts 26 Paul stood a prisoner for his faith before Festus, the Roman governor, and Herod Agrippa, the king. This was his opportunity to defend himself before a voyage to Rome and trial before Caesar. The old preacher did not argue—he simply testified. He went back to that day 26 years earlier when his best-laid plans came crashing down around him just outside Damascus. It was that hour when God said, "I want you. Come home—I have a job for you."

There is no evidence that God ever repeated that conversation with Paul. He did not have to. Once was enough. Wise is the man who, when God calls, gets up and answers. God may never call the same again.

So the aging preacher said, "Governor, your highness, that moment of conversion and that mission of service have controlled my life ever since. That vision has been my magnificent obsession. I was not disobedient to that heavenly vision. From the first day until now it has been my master motive, my single mission, my continuing message. That is the reason I stand before you now" (Acts 26:19, 22, author's paraphrase).

Notice closely the description in verse 22: "I continue unto this day, witnessing both to small and great, saying none other things than those which the prophets and Moses did say should come" (KJV). First, he says his message is *biblical*. He says nothing beyond what the prophets and Moses said would happen. Paul learns early what multitudes of Christian leaders and laity have discovered throughout the centuries: we have nothing to say beyond what God has already revealed in His Word.

Second, his message is Christ-centered (v. 23). He tells people about Christ and calls them to Christ. He preaches the good news of Christ's suffering, death, and resurrection for us. He calls Christ a light to his own people and a light to the Gentiles.

Third, he declares that his message is *life changing*. It calls for repentance toward God (v. 20), the validity of which is demonstrated in changed lives of holy living and good deeds.

It is amazing what power the people of God find in the faith once delivered to the saints. It is a power to stand before kings and governors. But more important, it is the power to live the Christian life in its purest simplicity over the long journey.

Well-known evangelist Billy Graham has modeled this power of God in our time. His life and message have been straightforward, simple, biblical, and uncompromising. In a feature story on Graham, *Time* magazine quoted him as saying, "We have to have some rule of law in theology as well as every other part of our lives. And the rule of our spiritual life is found in the Bible, which I believe was totally and completely inspired by God."[1]

When God speaks, He calls us to himself in ways that are always biblical, Christ-centered, and life changing. That is as true today as it was in those first hours of faith in the middle of the first century. Attempts to change the message, alter its direction, or lessen the demands of His call are destined to fail.

III. THE CONSISTENT MAN

Twenty-six years down his road of obedience, the old preacher has an audience like none he has ever had before. He is aware that he is standing before "small and great" (v. 22), but he cannot change the message, because God has changed the man. With courage born of the Holy Spirit, he gives witness to the marvelous grace of God and the transforming work of his Savior.

From all outward appearance it seems that Paul failed that day. Festus called him crazy—"out of your mind," saying, "Your great learning is driving you insane" (v. 24). And Herod Agrippa ridiculed Paul for the presumption that he could be converted in such a setting with such a presentation.

If the rulers are unbending in their unbelief, the rugged apostle is unbending in his faith. He is a committed man, an unshakable Christian with a steadfast purpose. Listen to his passionate response: "I pray God that not only you but all who are listening to me today may become what I am, except for these chains" (v. 29).

What an incredible commitment and glorious example! Paul heard God say, "I want you," and after Paul said yes he never turned back.

Another incredible example of commitment took place September 7, 1995, when one of major league baseball's historic records was broken as Cal Ripken Jr. of the Baltimore Orioles played in consecutive game number 2,131, breaking Lou Gehrig's record of 2,130 games without missing. Gehrig's record had stood since 1939, and most people assumed it would never be equaled. But they were wrong. Ripken began his record-setting streak on May 30, 1982. A month later he was moved from third base to shortstop.

Ripken's record is a testament to his strength, skill, conditioning, commitment, and good fortune. In paying tribute to the incredible achievement, *Sacramento Bee* sportswriter Mark Kreidler wrote, "Cal Ripken Jr. did something majestically and histori-cally ordinary Wednesday evening: He showed up for work."[2] In-deed he did. While Ripken has been toiling consistently at his task, no fewer than 517 starting shortstops have been used by the other 27 major league teams, and during the same period 3,712 major league players have gone on the disabled list. In an explanation that displayed humility and class, Ripken said, "I did not set out to get this record—I just go out to try and play."[3] (The remarkable achievement ended September 20, 1998, at 2,632 consecutive games, when Ripken decided it was time to end the streak and voluntarily withdrew himself from the lineup.)

God has something similar in mind when He says to us these gripping words: "I want you. Come; follow Me." He intends it for a lifetime. That is what we observe in the life of Paul. God speaks, and Paul responds, never changing until the day he dies.

I met Bob Benson in my junior year at Pasadena College when he transferred there from his hometown of Nashville. I was charmed by his Southern drawl, his dry humor, and his folksy wisdom. He introduced me to Southern gospel music, much of it printed by his family's business in Nashville. We linked up again in seminary, and when I graduated, he followed me as pastor of a little Christian church in Gunn City, Missouri. Graduation led him to a couple of brief pastorates, but in time he and his wife, Peg, and children were back in Nashville, where he became a vi-tal part of the family business, Benson Publishing Company. Those were dynamic days in the gospel music publishing field, and in time Bob became the president of the company. Things were going very well in many ways. He and the family were ac-tive in Nashville First Church of the Nazarene. Though his health was poor, as it always had been, he wrote much and spoke often to congregations and at retreats.

But there was a voice still tugging at Bob Benson's heart. He thought of it not as a new calling but as the fresh renewal of an old one. So early one Labor Day Monday, in the quiet of his study, he wrote the letter that would resign him from the presi-dency of his company and offer himself to God for whatever ser-vice he might fill—camps, retreats, conferences, college chapels, and some unforgettable writing. In those few years until his death in 1986, he touched our world for good and left a legacy of a life-challenging truth. For me, the following paragraphs written on that Monday morning are like the voice of the Holy Spirit.

I know *wherever* is a reckless word. There are no halfway houses on the road to *wherever*. I have to use it guardedly. Even now, I have not gone far enough for it to be a word that is really mine. But I would like to learn to live and believe so that *wherever* will hold no fears for me.

For one reason or another, I am not always a follower. Sometimes I am afraid to go. Sometimes my life is so good that I do not want to leave where I am. But when I have gone and when I have allowed it to become my word, I want to say to you unreservedly, *wherever is worth going.*

At times I have remained behind only to find myself surrounded with nothing. But sometimes I have also left all to go with Him and I have known His everything. And I am convinced that if I would always go, I would always be glad.

The quest—
Wherever it takes you—go;
Whichever the task—do it.
Whatever the burden—accept it;
Whenever it calls—answer it;
Whichever the lesson—learn it;
However dark the path—follow Him,
Because *wherever He takes you,*
It is worth it.[4]

When God speaks, He says, "I want you."

"I Have People on My Heart"
Acts 18:1-18

*T*he year was 1954. I had graduated from seminary and was going to Oakland, California, as a youth pastor. During this same time a 52-year-old salesman named Ray was on the road, trying to make a living. His résumé showed that he had sold everything from Florida real estate to paper cups. In 1954 he was selling restaurant equipment to the retail food industry. In his travels and among his clients, Ray was impressed with what he observed in the business of a couple of brothers in San Bernardino, California. It was a new and simple concept of a limited menu, fast service, and cheap prices. Ray persuaded those brothers to negotiate a deal with him that would allow him to launch a restaurant using their methods, style, menu, and name. On April 15, 1955, Ray opened his duplicate restaurant in Des Plaines, Illinois. The menu was remarkably simple and his prices reasonable: hamburgers were 15 cents, and cheeseburgers were 19 cents. Everything else was a dime: french fries, milk, milkshakes, root beer, orangeade, cola, and coffee. Three months later Ray opened his second restaurant, in Fresno, California. Six years later he bought out his San Bernardino partners for $2.7 million.

The salesman's name was Ray Kroc. The brothers were

Dick and Mac McDonald. And that single restaurant has grown into the largest restaurant chain in the world—McDonald's. The statistics are incredible and still rising. New McDonald's restaurants are constantly being built, and they can be found around the world. And it started with a dream.

When God speaks to us, He, too, is wanting to plant a dream. He is wanting to say to us in some vivid, compelling way, "I have people on My heart. Help Me reach them."

Frank Laubach, a gifted missionary of a former generation, wrote from his assignment in the Philippines in 1930, "If I throw these mind windows apart and say, 'God, what shall we think of now?' He answers always in some graceful, tender dream. And I know that God is love-hungry, for He is constantly pointing me to some dull dead soul which He has never reached and wistfully urges me to help him reach that stolid tight-shut mind."[1]

The apostle Paul would say, "Yes, that's the way, exactly the way, it was for me. God was always saying, 'I have people on My heart, right here where you are, Paul. Help Me reach them.'"

The chapter is Acts 18. The place is the Greek city of Corinth. The time is about A.D. 55, some 19 years after Paul's Damascus road conversion. The message was and is still today "When God speaks, He says, 'I have people on My heart. Help Me reach them.'"

I. A SITUATION TO BE UNDERSTOOD
(Acts 18:1-8)

After God came to Paul on that Damascus road with convicting, converting, cleansing, and commissioning power, there followed for Paul an extended period of quiet in Tarsus, perhaps as long as six or seven years. Why God would allow such a gifted servant to be out of service that long is puzzling. But God knew what He was doing, maturing and preparing His man for the years of ministry that were ahead. With Paul's Jewish brethren despising him as a traitor and his new Christian brothers suspecting him as a spy, God knew His man was not yet ready for prime time.

God is working even when we cannot see it and may not understand it. In such times it is our responsibility to trust and keep on trusting.

God allowed Moses to give up the luxury and comfort of the Egyptian palace for the loneliness of the barren desert in preparation for delivering His people home again. God allowed Joseph to endure an endless chain of misfortune in order to get him to the place where he could rescue God's people from starvation. God allowed Peter to talk loudly and fail pitifully in order that, Spirit-filled at last, he might be a credible spokesman for the mighty Savior. God allowed Charles Colson to tumble from the highest rungs of political power in order to show him the emptiness of pride and make him a persuasive voice of the truth of Christ to our day.

God's ways may be beyond our understanding at times, but time and eternity will reveal His fruitful purpose.

His ways were working on Paul in order to work with him. It was Barnabas, great-hearted Barnabas, who sought out Paul at Tarsus and brought him to Antioch to preach, teach, and disciple the new believers there (Acts 11). This powerful ministry lasted for a year, and Antioch became the place where the term "Christian" was first used.

It was at Antioch that the movement of Christian missions was born. God spoke to the fellowship, saying, "Set apart for me Barnabas and Saul for the work to which I have called them" (Acts 13:2). The people on God's heart became the people on their hearts. They obeyed. Acts 13 and 14 tell about the first mission journey in Asia Minor and the islands close by. The following journey took Paul into Europe and the cities of Philippi, Thessalonica, Berea, Athens, and finally Corinth.

Corinth was some city. Its location had made it one of the great trading and commercial centers of the ancient world. But Corinth had also gained a notorious reputation for its evil and immoral living. The thought of living like a Corinthian meant to live with drunken and immoral debauchery. The lifestyle of this city would be a challenge for the gospel and would put the transforming power of Christ to the test.

In Corinth Paul followed his pattern of worshiping in the synagogue and telling everyone who would listen that Jesus was indeed the Messiah of God. Later he would write back and remember, "I resolved to know nothing while I was with you except Jesus Christ and him crucified" (1 Cor. 2:2).

Whether that deep intensity was a reaction against his efforts at philosophical debate with the intellectuals of Athens, or just the fresh challenge of evangelism in a wicked city, the truth remains that Paul arrived in Corinth with a consuming passion to lead people to Jesus. The clarity of his teaching, the zeal of his spirit, the dynamic of his total commitment to his Lord bore fruit.

Crispus, one of the rulers of the synagogue, came to faith, as did his entire family (Acts 18:8). The same was true of Titius Justus, a Gentile whose hunger for God had first drawn him to the synagogue. God's man was doing God's work in God's way with God's Spirit, and Paul was producing a harvest for Him.

With Paul's success came opposition. He was finally thrown out of the synagogue and told not to come back and teach Jesus anymore. So with great boldness he moved next door—to Titius Justus's home. There he continued to preach to a larger and mixed congregation of both Jews and Gentiles. Continuing commitment resulted, and with it both heightened tension and rising anger, culminating in legal charges and civic confrontation (vv. 12-18).

Paul was certainly not unacquainted with that kind of opposition and persecution. He had been beaten and imprisoned in Philippi. He had been first praised, then stoned and left for dead in Lystra. It was not the kind of thing he enjoyed or wanted, but it was something he was willing to face and endure for his Lord. To be sure, as the situation became more explosive, he had to weigh the matter prayerfully and carefully ask himself, "Do I stay on, or do I give up and move out?"

This is the kind of question that raises itself in the hearts of Christians in all places, both pastors and laypersons. The Christian life can be difficult for everyone some of the time. The whole intent of the gospel is the transformation of people and situations. Both can fight the change tenaciously. When the resistance to Christ is rugged and the battle is hard, something cries out for an easier road and a gentler assignment. What does God say in times like this?

II. A MESSAGE TO BE HEARD
(Acts 18:9-10)

It is especially at times like this that God speaks. Interesting, isn't it, that God speaks to His people when life is most difficult? C. S. Lewis made the profound and true observation that "God whispers to us in our pleasures, speaks in our conscience, but shouts in our pains: it is His megaphone to rouse a deaf world."[2]

So God spoke to Paul at that crisis hour with strengthening words of encouragement and promise. Here is what He said to His man—and what He has a way of saying to us: "Do not be afraid; keep on speaking, do not be silent. For I am with you, and no one is going to attack and harm you, because I have many people in this city" (vv. 9-11). Paul stayed for a year and a half in Corinth, teaching the Word of God to the people.

Note first that God's plan is people. He is saying to His man, "Paul, you may not believe this and may not see this, but I have a lot of people here in Corinth, this wild, wicked, needy city. I have mothers and fathers and boys and girls who need to hear about Jesus. They are on My heart, Paul, and I want them on your heart." That was God's plan that troubled night, and that was the dream He planted in the heart of Paul.

Second, God promises presence and protection. "No one is going to attack and harm you" (v. 10). "It won't be like Lystra, where they turned on you and nearly killed you. It won't be like Philippi, where they whipped you and chained you until I set you free in an earthquake [Acts 16]. As tense as it is, I make this promise to you, Paul, that I will keep you safe here."

Third, God's directive is "Keep at it. Don't quit. Don't give up. Don't be silent, and don't be afraid" (see v. 9). With that kind of divine instruction, Paul finds a new surge of strength and vision. He continues for a year and a half, a longer ministry than He has had anywhere else up to that time. God grew a church through Paul in that wretched city.

God is always in the people business of redemption. The Church of Jesus Christ may not be the most glamorous institution in the eyes of a fallen world, but it's the most glorious institution in the world, because it's doing God's business of redemption.

Jesus declares, "I will build my church" (Matt. 16:18). God is still saying to those with ears to hear and hearts to obey, "I have lots of people right here. Help Me reach them. Help Me build My Church."

The Lord and Paul did build the church in Corinth—that wild, wicked city. 1 Cor. 6:9 catalogs the prospect list, and it is not impressive as a soil for potential saints—the immoral, idolaters, adulterers, male prostitutes, homosexuals, thieves, the greedy, drunkards, slanderers, and swindlers. This is the kind of paganism that can easily drain our hearts and shatter our vision. But God says to His man, "I have these people on My heart. Help Me reach them. I'll help you do it."

The record is remarkable. Paul stays, and Jesus comes. His grace does a marvelous work of change. So the preacher later writes to them, "And that is what some of you were. But you were washed, you were sanctified, you were justified in the name of the Lord Jesus Christ and by the Spirit of our God" (1 Cor. 6:11).

To be sure, there are times when God says to move on and work elsewhere. But if we listen closely on our journey, we will hear Him say to us, "I have people on My heart right here where you are. Help Me reach them."

I was born in Anaheim, California, when it was a small town in the middle of endless orange groves—before Disneyland and Angel Stadium. The big adventure for my family in those early days was to travel six miles to neighboring Santa Ana to buy groceries and do other shopping. Santa Ana was some kind of town, with both a Sears and a Montgomery Ward. The drive took us down Placentia Avenue (where Angel Stadium now stands) to Manchester Boulevard and into Santa Ana.

At some point in my childhood a lot of orange trees were taken out of the intersection of Placentia and Manchester and a drive-in theater, surrounded by a high corrugated iron fence, was built. I remember wondering, as we made that turn, what went on inside that place. If it was nighttime, I strained my neck to catch a momentary glance of the forbidden movies.

In the same year that I was graduating from seminary and Ray Kroc was dreaming of his golden arches, a young pastor in Chicago was asked by his denomination to leave his comfortable parish and move to southern California to establish a new church in Orange County. It was just after Christmas when he arrived with his wife and a handful of possessions.

For a month he searched for a place to conduct services but found none. With the population explosion that was taking place at that time in that area, every denomination was pioneering a new work. The new pastor tried the mortuary, the lodge, even the Seventh-day Adventist Church, but all were taken. The only place he discovered available was the drive-in theater at the corner of Placentia and Manchester.

Local ministers laughed at the new kid on the block. But Robert Schuller believed he had found the door that God had opened, and he would walk through it.

Sunday morning, March 27, 1955, at 11 A.M. Schuller stood for the first time on a makeshift platform and spoke into a microphone that carried the sound of his voice to the speakers in the few cars that had gathered for the first service of his "drive-in church." It was not a glamorous beginning, but Dr. Schuller had caught the sound of the voice and dream of God: "I have people on My heart here. Help Me reach them."

Today Garden Grove's Crystal Cathedral ministers each Sunday to 6,000 to 8,000 people on its grounds and touches lives around the world via television, literature, and conferences.

How many times as a child and a young person I had driven by that intersection and had seen only orange groves and a drive-in movie place! But another man of God saw in it the beginnings of one of the great works of God. Now, more than 40 years later, Dr. Schuller is still at it, as if the words of God are still in his ear: "Do not be afraid. Keep on speaking. I am with you. I have many people in this city."

III. A Truth to Be Applied

God is still saying to His people today what He said to Paul. If we listen closely we will catch His words: "I have people on My heart. Help Me reach them."

I have heard Him say them to me, and His words become the heart of my ministry and my focus of living. Sometimes we yearn for other messages from the Lord, but this message is enduring, though not always easy. The "go" of God is so often against the grain of our fallen world. Like the people of Corinth, we find things in life to be frustrating and discouraging. But to obey and endure—to build the bridges of faith to others in Jesus' name—is to experience the deep blessing that comes from our obedience to God. Immeasurable joy can fill us up, knowing another person has returned to God's forever family.

I have come to believe that if God has a favorite word, it is "come." This is His word again and again throughout the Scripture, calling out to people who are on His heart. To be sure, it is not His only word, but it is His special word. That's what He said through Isaiah the prophet. To the wayward He said, "Come now, let us reason together. . . . Though your sins are like scarlet, they shall be as white as snow; though they are red as crimson, they shall be like wool" (Isa. 1:18).

To the broken He says, "Come, all you who are thirsty, come to the waters; and you who have no money, come, buy and eat! Come, buy wine and milk without money and without cost. Why spend money on what is not bread, and your labor on what does not satisfy?" (Isa. 55:1-2)

This is God's word through His Son, our Lord Jesus Christ. This is what He says personally to Peter as He invites him into a new, life-changing walk of faith: "Come, follow me" (Mark 1:17).

This is what Jesus says to all people: "Come to me, all you who are weary and burdened, and I will give you rest. Take my yoke upon you and learn from me, for I am gentle and humble in heart, and you will find rest for your souls. For my yoke is easy and my burden is light" (Matt. 11:28-30).

That beautiful word, "come," is God's final word in the Scriptures. On the last page, in the last chapter of Revelation, God speaks to the world His word of invitation and calls the redeemed to participate with Him: "The Spirit and the bride say, 'Come!' And let him who hears say, 'Come!' Whosoever is thirsty, let him come" (Rev. 22:17).

When God talks to us about the people on His heart, He is inviting us to share in His efforts to reach them with His love. When our lives are in His hands, then His call becomes a part of our hearts.

The late Howard Hamlin was an outstanding surgeon and a remarkable Christian layman. His Christian commitment moved him toward missions in post-World War II China early in his life, but the Communist takeover slammed shut that door of potential ministry. His medical practice and career in Chicago was everything a doctor could ever desire. He was loved and respected, caring for both the rich and the famous as well as the ordinary people of his city. His churchmanship elevated him to the highest levels of church leadership. When his church called him to Swaziland to fill an urgent hospital need, he immediately resigned his thriving practice to answer the call.

Dr. Hamlin's action was reported on page 1 of the *Chicago Tribune*. On reading the news, a longtime friend, a Jewish neurosurgeon named Josh, phoned and asked, "Howard, are you nuts? . . . Do you know what you're doing?"

Dr. Hamlin's answer was classic Christian: "Yes, Josh, in the words of one of your great forebears, the apostle Paul, 'the love of Christ constrains me.' "[3]

It would be easy to point to the Robert Schullers and the Howard Hamlins of the Christian faith and declare them as representative of what God expects of all Christians. Obviously this is not true. God does not call us to fame or success—but to faithfulness. And faithfulness will put us in that relationship with Him where we hear His voice saying those words about people on His heart, asking us to help Him build a bridge of faith from Him to them.

Stephanie and Nathan shared the same seventh grade class in a small school just outside town in the Sierra foothills of northern California. Stephanie and her family were members of our church. Nathan and his family were not attending anywhere, until Stephanie invited him to attend church with her one Sunday. This became the beginning of another wonderful chapter in God's book about reaching people on His heart.

Nathan's mother, Linda, and her sister, Pam, had been brought up in a home that was devout but not Evangelical Christian. Neither Linda's agnostic husband, Ron, nor Pam's gregarious husband, Allen, had time for the church or interest in the Lord. But Linda and Pam had the hunger of mothers wanting to point their children toward God. The church of their childhood was too far away, and occasional efforts to attend were frustrating. They decided to try the church where Nathan had been invited.

I remember the first Sunday they came, Pam with her four children and Linda with her six; each mother carried a newborn infant in her arms. Neither husband was present.

In a short time, the Holy Spirit drew Pam and Linda into the circle of saving faith in Jesus and into the fellowship of the church. The fathers eventually came to see what was going on. In time, Ron and Allen joined Linda, Pam, and the children in declaring Christ as their Lord. In the end, these two families became leaders of the church, examples of what it means to live as God's people.

Nathan grew up, married, and has entered the Christian ministry with his wife, Carmen. Nathan's sister Kaitlin and her husband, Mike, are also serving in Christian ministry. All of this is because a seventh grade girl invited a classmate to Sunday School and church.

I hear God say these words again, the same ones He said to Paul. Listen closely and you will hear Him say them to you: "Do not be afraid; keep on speaking, do not be silent . . . because I have many people in this city" (vv. 9-10). Indeed, He has people on His heart.

"I Have Something Else in Mind"

Acts 22:17-21

The year is 1735, 115 years after the Pilgrims landed at Plymouth and began their holy adventure in the New World. A young man named John Wesley is a 32-year-old teaching fellow at Oxford University's Lincoln College. His preacher father had just passed away, and John and his brothers had succeeded in publishing their late father's massive work on the Book of Job.

John went to London to present a copy of the book to Queen Caroline. While there, he met General Oglethorpe, the founder of what was known as "the Savannah experiment" in the colony of Georgia.

The general's motivation for the experiment came from his passionate reform of English jails and his philanthropic compassion for the debtors who had been harshly imprisoned. At the point of his meeting John Wesley, Oglethorpe was in the process of looking for a priest for the colony—the third in three years. The first had died soon after his arrival in Georgia, and the second had been asked to leave. Oglethorpe invited John Wesley to become the minister at Savannah.

John returned home and asked for a leave of absence from Oxford. With his godly mother's blessing, he set sail for America October 14, 1735. His 27-year-old brother Charles accompanied him. Susanna, his mother, declared, "Had I 20 sons, I should rejoice that they were all so employed, though I should see them no more."

The move from Oxford to Savannah looked so right and sounded so good. But history records that for the Wesleys it was an expedition of shattered dreams and disappointing failures. In a few short months Charles headed home, never to return. Twenty months after he landed, John also returned to England, leaving behind no Indian converts nor even a blazing light of gospel truth. The only specific account left for telling is about his halfhearted romance with Sophey Hopkey, which ended with a defamation of character suit against the jealous young priest.

One wonders what might have happened if John Wesley had married Sophey Hopkey—if John and Charles had been success-ful in their mission to America. What impact might they have had through long-term ministry to the pardoned prisoners and native Indians? The truth is that *God had something else in mind.*

God took the dismal record of ministry in America and used it as part of a preparation for a better plan. He overhauled the young preacher with a conversion that gave him the gospel message and the fullness of the Holy Spirit, investing him with spiritual power to touch England with revival, and the Christian world has been grateful ever since.

This adventure of John Wesley reflects a time when another preacher went off on a mission filled with godly dreams of blessed service, only to have those dreams interrupted by God himself, who said, "I have something else in mind."

Paul tells it best in his own words:

> When I returned to Jerusalem and was praying at the temple, I fell into a trance and saw the Lord speaking. "Quick!" he said to me. "Leave Jerusalem immediately, be-cause they will not accept your testimony about me."
>
> "Lord," I replied, "these men know that I went from one synagogue to another to imprison and beat those who be-lieve in you. And when the blood of your martyr Stephen was shed, I stood there giving my approval and guarding the clothes of those who were killing him."
>
> Then the Lord said to me, "Go; I will send you far away to the Gentiles" *(Acts 22:17-21).*

This is the language of God. When God speaks, in addition to "I want you" and "I have people on My heart" He may also say, "I have something else in mind."

1. The Surprising Announcement from God

"God said, 'Quick! . . . Leave Jerusalem immediately'" (v. 18).

If this announcement does not surprise you, you need to understand that it certainly surprised Paul. The event of which Paul spoke occurred some 22 years before he related it to an angry crowd in the courtyard of the Temple. It is interesting that this is Paul's only reference to that crucial moment of his Christian journey—a journey that flows so swiftly in Scripture. For the sake of keeping Paul's journey in perspective, it might be helpful to take a quick review of his Christian life up to this point.

It began one day on the road outside of Damascus about A.D. 36. The Christian faith was new, only a few years beyond the crucifixion, resurrection, and ascension of Jesus Christ.

Paul, a cruel foe of Christianity, had gone to Damascus with papers of authority to track down, arrest, and carry back to Jerusalem any Christians he could discover. This was the plan of the mean-spirited Pharisee; but God had something else in mind.

In a dramatic conversion, the least likely person of the first century became a Christian. In a moment, in the grip of conviction, Paul was transformed into a new creature. Through the personal ministry of Ananias (a believer) and the very Christians he had intended to harm, Paul was nurtured in those crucial first days of faith (Acts 9).

In the second part of Paul's journey, according to Gal. 1:15-17, Paul leaves Damascus for Arabia. This episode is mentioned only in Galatians. The purpose of this time of quietness was to help Paul better understand what was happening in his life and to form a theology that would explain and account for his transformed life.

While Acts 9 does not mention it, some Bible scholars believe that after a fair length of time in Arabia, Paul returned to Damascus and began to share his faith. (Paul also states in Gal. 1:17 that after spending time in Arabia he returned to Damascus.) This began the third stage of his ministry.

Paul's testimony was more polished and his theology more compelling than in the beginning, and resentment against him grew in the Jewish community. With a price on his head, Paul escaped when friends lowered him in a basket over the city wall at night. (2 Cor. 11:32-33 suggests that even Aretas, the Nabatean king of Arabia, had taken offense to Paul as well.)

Paul returns to Jerusalem, in the fourth stage of his journey. Gal. 1:18 tells us that this was after three years. This time it is to exalt the Savior he once was out to destroy. If Paul has high hopes, which he surely must have had, they are quickly quenched with the cold water of bitter reality. The Christians in Jerusalem are suspicious of their former foe and his newfound words of faith. The Jews in Jerusalem show nothing but contempt for the one, who in his defection to Christ, has betrayed the cause that he once set out to defend. However, it is the friendship of Barnabas, blessed Barnabas the encourager, that radically transforms the response of the Christian community from suspicion and uncertainty to acceptance and joy. Nothing, however, can soothe the boiling resentment of Paul's former Jewish brothers.

Paul's time in Jerusalem is brief; only 15 days, according to Gal. 1:18. It is here, just a couple of weeks into the grand dream of a new Christian, that God confronts Paul as he prays in the Temple. The words are blunt and urgent: "Quick! . . . Leave Jerusalem immediately, because they will not accept your testimony about me" (v. 18).

That was it. God's word: "Leave." God's reason: "They will not listen." God had something else in mind.

Will God really interrupt our well-made plans to challenge us with another agenda on His mind? Scripture makes it quite clear that He can and He has.

There are many examples. Abraham was quite comfortable in Haran. Joseph did not mind at all being the favored son of his aging father. Moses had come to accept his forlorn fate with the sheep on the sparse edge of the desert. David was quite happy being a free-spirit, guitar-playing shepherd. Peter, Andrew, James, and John had every intention of being lifelong fishermen, just like their fathers, and their fathers' fathers before them.

But in every case God comes with other plans. He does not always announce it, but He is doing it just the same. If God is God, and if we are even slightly interested in being His, then He has the right to come to us and say, "This is what I have in mind." God's plan may be different from what *we* had in mind, but it will be better than we had planned.

II. THE INTERESTING ARGUMENT WITH GOD

Paul, the young Christian just three years old in Christ, was obviously surprised by the directive from God. So he argued, saying, "Lord . . . these men know that I went from one synagogue to another to imprison and beat those who believe in you. And when the blood of your martyr Stephen was shed, I stood there giving my approval and guarding the clothes of those who were killing him" (vv. 19-20).

In Paul's youthful vision, Jerusalem was the place to be, giving his testimony, sharing his faith, and witnessing to former friends and foes alike. What an opportunity to say, "This is what happened to me, and this is what I now believe." In essence his argument against the directive of God ran this way: "But, Lord, these people know me; and because they know me, they will listen to me."

It is difficult to find fault with either Paul's logic or his zeal. He was right on target in so many ways. He had big plans for the Lord in the big city. But two things are missing in Paul's thinking. The first is his inability to measure the deep hatred of those who opposed him. They were having a hard time understanding his changed life or his Christian faith. To them, Paul's betrayal of their heritage was unforgivable treason and blasphemy.

The second missing item in Paul's thinking is his unawareness of God's greater plan. God wanted his servant not just for a short witness in Jerusalem but for decades of ministry throughout the empire. This extended ministry would never have happened if Paul had carried out his own plan.

God does not always announce to us the reasons for the things that happen in life. To our limited minds, many of the events of our lives seem random and senseless. But with eyes of faith, we can look back and clearly see that when it looked as though God was letting down His people, He was leading them on.

Joseph must have wrestled with all the bitter things that damaged his bright dreams—from the hatred of his brothers to the false accusations of Potiphar's wife and the years of confining imprisonment. These events must have weighed on him with crushing oppression. He might have asked a thousand times, "Where's God?"

But the same providence that allowed those bitter times in Joseph's life also brought the brighter unfolding of the better plan of God. From his powerful position in Egypt, Joseph could joyfully testify to his brothers, "You intended to harm me, but God intended it for good to accomplish what is now being done, the saving of many lives" (Gen. 50:20).

Billy Graham has become a model Christian for millions, including me. The integrity of his life, the consistency of his message, and the harvest of his preaching are evidence of the hand of God upon him.

When Graham was a 20-year-old ministerial student at Florida Bible Institute, his roommate introduced him to an attractive, intelligent, devout young female student, Emily Cavanaugh. Billy fell head over heels in love with her and told his roommate she was the girl he was going to marry. But Emily had other ideas and broke off the relationship. She was concerned about his immaturity and lack of purpose; she wanted to marry a man who was going to amount to something. This rejection was a time of emotional devastation for Graham as his world seemed shattered. In time, this turn of events nurtured in Graham a deeper commitment to Christ than he had ever known.[1]

What if Emily Cavanaugh had said yes to Billy Graham? Would the things he had planned with such good intentions have thwarted God's greater plan with a lovely young lady named Ruth Bell and long decades of supportive marriage, nurturing love, and remarkable ministry? Indeed, God had something better in mind.

III. THE UNFOLDING ASSIGNMENT OF GOD

Then the Lord says to Paul, "Go; I will send you far away to the Gentiles" (v. 21). The immediate issue is safety. God, as the great economist, is not about to needlessly lose a key player. He has done too much to bring to this place this man least likely to serve God. God does not want to lose him.

The second issue for Paul is his ministry. God's great plan for Paul includes a field as wide as the empire itself. This plan includes the formulation of Christian doctrine and the evangelizing of the Mediterranean world that would build a bridge to the non-Jewish world—and to us.

So off to Tarsus Paul goes, to the great city of Cilesia. For the next six years, God's man greatly matures. Though the details of those years are not recorded, Paul must have learned how to share Jesus Christ with people of every culture. Because when revival broke out in Antioch and Barnabas needed assistance in discipling the converts, he knew Paul was the man for the task. Barnabas searched Tarsus for Paul, until he found him, and from that day on it was full speed ahead for the Lord.

This is the way it is. God says, "I have something else in mind." Paul finally agrees, yields to God and to an agenda he does not yet understand, and God accomplishes His better plan.

As we apply this way to our lives, there are some truths we need to identify. First, we need to declare that God does not always decide our plans are wrong. What chaos would prevail in our lives if all the intentions of our best thinking were interrupted! The promise of Prov. 3:5-6 is that as we trust in the Lord, He will direct our paths. More often than not, daily obedience, sanctified judgment, and a continuing hunger to know and do the will of God will find us right where He wants us. It would be a distortion of the text to think that my Christian plans and desires are always wrong.

However, the truth remains that God has the right at any time in life to interrupt plans of our own with His plans. It is not likely to happen daily, but His interruption will likely happen sometime.

Bill Gothard has vividly taught the Christian world that at some point there has to be a death of our dreams if there is to be the discovery of God's better dream. Paul examples this for us as he dies to his dream for Jerusalem, for God's greater dream for the world.

It is when our plans have fallen apart and God's full intention and agenda have not yet been revealed and achieved that we are called upon to wait and trust. Twenty years elapsed before Paul could see the wisdom of God's interruption and the urgent departure from Jerusalem. Those six years of seemingly wasted time in Tarsus must have been trying and frustrating. But in His time God makes things plain. When we cannot see, we must believe. When we cannot understand, we must trust.

Hoyt Stone was a teenager when he shared with his pastor father and his church that he had been called to preach. One Sunday his father announced that his son would preach in the following Sunday night service. All week Hoyt alternated between paralyzing fear and fantasies of adolescent glory. Perhaps he would become the new spellbinder of the gospel world, he dreamed, as he chose his text and prepared himself for his debut. Hoyt let his thoughts wander into how his pastor-father might handle the greater adulation the congregation would probably heap on his gifted son.

Then it was time to speak. When Hoyt stood up, everything left him. In the grip of panic that sometimes visits the pulpit, Hoyt started, stammered, prayed, started over, stammered, and prayed again. After the fourth false start, his father took over, and Hoyt hurried out the back door of the church.

Hoyt felt he had made a fool of himself. In embarrassment, he later left for college without ever attempting to preach again. In college he studied, read, worked, took a speech course, and looked at himself closely. He knew that he would never again stand before a congregation without adequate preparation and without something to say.

Further down the road of Hoyt's life he would write, "Years later it came to me how fortunate I was to have failed in that first sermon."[2]

How much this is like God! In His own way and in His own time He clarifies His better plan to those who dare to follow Him.

If you are now at some point of unplanned and unexplained interruption, you can take courage and believe that God has something else in mind for you—and His plan is always better.

"I Have Plans for You"

Acts 23:1-22

$\mathcal{T}$he world into which my parents were born, around the start of the 1900s, was a different world in many ways from the one they left 74 and 87 years later. Their world changed on them—from rural farm to busy city; from horse and buggy transportation to luxury automobiles and jet airplanes; from home remedies to modern medicine; from kerosene lamps to electric lights; from a tiny world no larger than their Missouri village to a whole world in their living room, first through radio and then through television.

It's true: the only thing that does not change is change itself. Even wise Solomon warned, "Do not boast about tomorrow, for you do not know what a day may bring forth" (Prov. 27:1). But this is not the whole story. *The Lord* does not change. This is what He boldly declares to the prophet Malachi: "I the LORD do not change" (Mal. 3:6). In Him are some constants to which we can cling and on which we can build. While none of us knows tomorrow, we can, as has often been preached, know Him who holds our tomorrows and trust Him to lead us where we have not yet been.

When God speaks, what does He say? The apostle Paul tells us of a frightening time in his life when God speaks the exciting words "I have plans for you."

I. ENCOURAGEMENT IN THE MIDST OF FAILURE

Once again it's night when God speaks to Paul, though God is certainly not limited to nighttime communication (as if He calls only when telephone rates are lower). After all, it was high noon when He shattered Paul's comfortable but mean world on the Damascus road with that inescapable ultimatum "I want you." But for whatever reason, half of the recorded conversations of God with Paul occurred at night.

It is interesting—at night, when our strength is at its lowest, when the silence can be deafening, when life's problems can be magnified a thousand times, when fears can overwhelm and paralyze, when the noise of life is quieted and the tempo of life slows to a crawl—the still, small voice of God can be heard if we listen.

For Paul this is not just any night. It is a dreadful night filled with terrifying uncertainty, a night when nerves are raw and sleep impossible. It is the old preacher's second night in jail.

Paul's return from his third missionary journey has been filled with great expectation. He brings with him a company of selected men from the churches where he has ministered, and with them a generous offering for the mother church in Jerusalem. How could anything so good turn out so wrong? While Paul had experienced intuitions of difficulty ahead (Acts 20:22), he had been assured of God's presence and strength.

How quickly things had seemed to sour! Rumors quickly spread that Paul had taken his Gentile Christian friend Trophimus into the Temple with him (21:28). These false accusations inflame a mob who, in a frenzy of religious rage, seize the apostle and beat him, intending to kill him (vv. 26-32). Deliverance comes from law enforcement—the captain of the Roman guard and his soldiers. Paul's arrest becomes his rescue.

Paul seizes the opportunity to testify as he is marched up the steps to the prison barracks overlooking the Temple courtyard. With the commander's permission, the apostle quiets the crowd below, then takes them back to his former days when he was exactly as they were—zealous, narrow, and angry. He directs them back to noontime near Damascus when the Jesus he had hated transformed his life and sent him on a gospel mission to Gentiles as well as Jews. The mention of the Gentiles does not go over well, and their rage erupts again. The commander and his men jail Paul for the night.

The next day, at Paul's arraignment before the Jewish legislature, he fares no better. They, too, would have torn him apart (23:10). Once again the captain and his men forcefully rescue Paul and march him back to jail.

The old preacher, Paul, is no coward. He has suffered for his Lord before, and he would suffer again. He had the premonition that this assignment would not be easy, but he is human just as we're all human. He knows what it's like to do his best and receive hatred instead of appreciation, a slap in the face and rejection instead of a pat on the back.

When this negative feedback occurs, the spirit struggles. And this is the night when it happens for Paul. When his spirits have sunk to the bottom and there seems no way out, the Lord comes and stands near him and speaks. His word is a message of encouragement in the middle of failure.

"Take courage!" God simply says (23:11).

How like God to be there when we're down! There's nothing trivial about His words, and He does not ramble on. When we need Him most, He is simply present. "When other helpers fail and comforts flee," He comes to let us know He has not forgotten and is not finished.

The word "encouragement" literally means to give heart, and when God speaks He gives heart—because we need it. Just as Eliphaz said to Job, "Your words have kept men on their feet" (Job 4:4, MOFFATT), how much more God wants to use our voices to become His voice with words of heart.

It is a privilege to tell someone on the raw edges of life that God has not forgotten and God will not abandon. "God has said, 'Never will I leave you; never will I forsake you'" (Heb. 13:5).

On the day after Christmas one year I felt I needed to write a short note of encouragement to a pastor friend who was going through a dark time in his life. In exactly nine months I received a reply. He said in his letter, "Before me is a letter of encouragement that you wrote last December 26. I wanted to take this moment to thank you for caring so much when life was really tough last fall and for almost a year. Your words brought comfort and lifted my soul. It is so good to know that someone really shares our heartache in an hour of need." If my letter helped him, I know his letter helped me.

II. A PROMISE IN THE MIDST OF THREATENING UNCERTAINTY

God speaks, saying, "Take courage! As you have testified about me in Jerusalem, so you must also testify in Rome" (v. 11).

What a promise! In his humanity, all Paul can think about is getting through the night. He knows that his life is not worth a dime in Jerusalem; two close calls have established that. There really seems no way out. But then God comes and slightly parts the curtain of tomorrow. He lets His man know that it's not over. Jerusalem is not the end, only a point on the journey. God still has plans for Paul—an assignment at the very heart of the empire.

A ministry in Rome has been Paul's growing desire and dream. Not long before, in Ephesus, when Paul's soul was growing restless and he was packing for his trip to Jerusalem, he had a dream of getting to Rome. He told those early Christians, "After I have been there [Jerusalem] . . . I must visit Rome also" (Acts 19:21).

Exactly what Paul had in mind is not clear. But when Jerusalem collapses into chaos and everything seems finished, God "stood near" to say, "I am still here. You have a future. I have plans for you at the very heart of the empire. At Rome, where Caesar rules and all roads lead, there you will testify for Me."

Marguerite Higgins is a former Pulitzer prizewinning correspondent from the Korean War era. She filed a story of the Fifth Company of United States Marines in outnumbered battle with more than 100,000 Chinese Communist soldiers. That particular morning was terribly cold, 42 degrees below zero. Weary troops, their clothes crusted with mud and stiff as boards, were eating cold beans from tin cans with trench knives. Higgins asks one marine what he would want more than anything else if she were God and could grant his request. He stood motionless for a moment, then answered, "Give me tomorrow."[1]

Is God really in the business of giving us tomorrows? I believe He is. The situation for Paul seems to say, "It's over." But God says, "How about Rome?"

The psalmist puts God's promise in other words: "Delight yourself in the LORD and he will give you the desires of your heart" (Ps. 37:4).

We must understand God correctly. There will come a time when His tomorrow for us will be not here on earth, but there with Him. Still, God is One who always wants to say yes. "The man who does the will of God lives forever" (1 John 2:17). The promises of God are "Yes" in Christ (see 2 Cor. 1:20).

God did not tell Paul everything. He parted the curtain of the future only slightly—just enough to declare a promise and to ignite a sense of courage. God did not tell Paul that he would go as a prisoner, that he would endure two years in a Palestinian jail before he arrived. God did not disclose the fact that Paul's ministry in Rome would be under house arrest and that eventually he would die as a martyr for Christ.

God was saying to Paul the same thing He is saying to us: "I have plans for you. Don't give up, and don't go back. I'm not finished, and neither are you."

The people of Judah in the time of Jeremiah were going through some terrible days. The sins of the people had brought them to an hour of reckoning. Babylon was tearing the nation apart. But God in mercy had a promise for His people. It was the promise of a tomorrow.

"This is what the LORD says: 'When seventy years are completed for Babylon, I will come to you and fulfill my gracious promise to bring you back to this place. For I know the plans I have for you,' declares the LORD, 'plans to prosper you and not to harm you, plans to give you hope and a future. Then you will call upon me and come and pray to me, and I will listen to you.

You will seek me and find me when you seek me with all your heart'" (Jer. 29:10-13).

God is dreaming and planning the best for those who will hear and honor Him.

When 23-year-old Bill Bright moved from his home in Coweta, Oklahoma, to Los Angeles in 1944, he had plans to set up his own business: Bright's California Confections. His products included such things as fruits, jams, jellies, and candy. Little did he anticipate what God had in mind for him. In a series of providential events, Bright was brought into contact with Louis Evans Sr., pastor of the First Presbyterian Church of Hollywood, and the gifted and dynamic Henrietta Mears, the leader of the college-and-career youth group at the church.

In spring 1945 Bright made a life-changing commitment to Jesus Christ. Determined to learn all he could about his new faith, he enrolled in Princeton Seminary in the fall of 1946. But he soon returned to southern California and became a part of the first class of the new Fuller Theological Seminary in Pasadena. Through Miss Mears's "Fellowship of the Burning Heart," his commitment to Christ deepened to a full consecration. His business interest faded as his spiritual journey captured him. Bright married Vonette Zachary in 1948. Together they chose to abandon worldly achievement and to be everything the Lord wanted them to be. They even wrote out a contract with the Lord in which they took on the status of slaves to Jesus Christ.

In spring 1951 Bright was studying for final exams at Fuller. That night God came to him in an unusual way and gave him a vision of a ministry that would touch our world. That ministry we know today as Campus Crusade for Christ and its goal is to "win the campus to Christ today, win the world to Christ tomorrow." Bright dropped out of seminary, counseled with respected leaders, and launched his first campus ministry at the University of California at Los Angeles in the fall of 1951. Five years later he wrote "The Four Spiritual Laws" booklet as a witnessing tool for the Crusade staff.

Today Campus Crusade for Christ is a dynamic and marvelous Christian ministry that employs 14,200 staff members and coordinates 163,000 volunteers in 167 countries. Over 1 billion copies of "The Four Spiritual Laws" have been printed. It is estimated that Campus Crusade for Christ has reached at least 2 billion people with the gospel. What a miraculous harvest from a late-night word from God, who said to a 30-year-old man, "I have plans for you."[2]

III. HELP IN THE MIDST OF GREAT CRISIS

Paul's ordeal does not end at dawn, despite the presence and promise of God. The new day brings another episode of anxiety. No fewer than 40 men had plotted to neither eat nor drink until they had killed Paul (vv. 12-22). The conspiracy even included those in religious leadership and in the legislature (vv. 14-15), making Paul's situation, once again, look hopeless.

What good is God's promise against odds like that? The answer is that *God is always as good as His word.* He will fulfill His plan.

In remarkable providence, Paul's nephew overhears the plot and informs Paul and the commander. With utmost precaution, guarded by a detachment of nearly 500 soldiers, Paul is transferred by night to the prison at the territorial capital of Caesarea. God is backing His Word with this action. It is as if He is saying, "Paul, I have a plan for you, and I will get you to Rome. Not all the devils of hell can keep us from it."

Through all that was to come, the promise of God in the night was the hope, encouragement, and guarantee that held God's man steady in the storm. Does God really do that? The Bible says He does. And the people of God across the centuries have testified that in His own way and in His own time, He does.

How, then, do we apply this word from God to our lives? We begin by remembering that there are some things that are a part of God's plan for all of us. They are clearly revealed and consistently taught in His Word.

First, His plan for us is to *know Him personally* in the reality of the grace of Jesus Christ, grace that both justifies freely and sanctifies wholly. This plan is for everyone—you and me and the man next door. 2 Pet. 3:9 declares that God does not want "anyone to perish, but everyone to come to repentance." His plan starts here.

Second, God's plan is for us to *serve Him faithfully.* Paul would later write from that Roman imprisonment, "For to me, to live is Christ" (Phil. 1:21).

This is not an alternative plan of God—it is *the* plan of God. To be out of God's will spiritually is to be out of God's plan personally.

Third, God's plan is for us to *share Him fruitfully.* He wants us to be His bridges to others, His light for our dark world, and His love for our lonely and lost world. Jesus says, "You did not choose me, but I chose you and appointed you to go and bear fruit—fruit that will last" (John 15:16). This is what God wants—the life of Christ in us lovingly, intentionally, and prayerfully reproduced in others. These things are God's plan for everyone.

But God also has a plan specifically designed for each of us. He is engaged in working out that plan as we live in Him. We may see only a part of it at any given time. But we live in the assurance that God is at work where God is at home.

To the church in Rome, where God promised Paul he would one day minister, the apostle wrote with deep assurance, "We know that in all things God works for the good of those who love him, who have been called according to His purpose" (Rom. 8:28). To the faithful in Philippi Paul wrote with both challenge and assurance, "Therefore, my dear friends, as you have always obeyed—not only in my presence, but now much more in my absence—continue to work out your salvation with fear and trembling, for it is God who works in you to will and to act according to his good purpose" (Phil. 2:12-13).

When we don't know everything and cannot see the whole plan, it is then that we must do what is clearly at hand, believing that God will reveal the next step in His own time and way.

In the opening of John Bunyan's *Pilgrim's Progress,* there is a compelling moment in which Christian is asking the Evangelist for directions to God and glory. As the Evangelist points with his finger over a wide field, he asks, "Do you see yonder wicket-gate?"

Christian says, "No."

Then the Evangelist asks, "Do you see yonder shining light?"

Christian answers, "I think I do."

And he was given this instruction: "Keep that light in your eye, and go up directly thereto; so shalt thou see the gate; at which when thou knockest, it shall be told thee what thou shalt do."³

God says, "I have a plan for you." When we cannot see all of it, we must hold on to what we can see until more of it is revealed.

"You Can Make It"

Acts 27:13-26

*H*e came into my office and slumped into the chair, burying his face into his callused mechanic's hands. In a few moments Marvin looked up and said, "Pastor, I don't know what to do. My situation is beyond me." Then he began to cry softly, something his burly disposition would never have allowed him to do, and whispered hoarsely, "I'm totally helpless."

I sat in silence, moved by the intensity of Marvin's desperation. Then I said in an answer that I believe now was inspired then by the Holy Spirit, "Marvin, it may be that at this very moment God is doing His best work in you."

What does God say when we come to the end of ourselves, when our best-laid plans seem to have collapsed and our hardest efforts are going nowhere? I have come to believe that if we have ears to hear, we will hear God saying to us in that dark and difficult hour, "You can make it. Don't give up."

This is exactly what God said to the apostle Paul one desperate, seemingly hopeless night. These words were there, when it appeared that life was over—when there seemed to be no way out—that God came and spoke those blessed words of assurance, "You can make it." In the precious redemptive vocabulary of God, these words are still being said. If you listen closely, you will hear Him speak those marvelous words to you.

I. Man's Exhausting Predicament

Paul's excited return to Jerusalem from his third mission journey had turned into a soured chain of unplanned, unwanted, and uncontrollable events. From the threatened lynching by a mob in the Temple courtyard (Acts 22) to two long years of frustrating imprisonment in the Roman provincial capital of Caesarea, it had to be one of the darkest periods of Paul's Christian life. Before the new Roman governor, Festus, Paul had appealed his case to Rome (chap. 26). He wanted the thing settled. He wanted his name cleared of false charges. He wanted his freedom. He wanted to continue his ministry.

This was the reason for the voyage to Rome and Caesar. Paul the prisoner was committed to the keeping of a Roman centurion named Julius. Luke was allowed to go along as Paul's attending physician. (The "we" passages that begin in Acts 16 and cease at the end of chap. 21 resume again in chap. 27, indicating the personal presence of Luke the writer.) Luke wrote with the vividness of an eyewitness, because he *was* one. Aristarchus was also accompanying them (27:2). He was a believer from Thessalonica who had made the journey with Paul to Jerusalem to deliver the love offering from the emerging Gentile church to the saints at Jerusalem (20:4).

Luke records the voyage well. It takes them up the coast of Israel, then westward under the shoreline of Asia Minor to the port of Myra. Changing vessels, they board a grain ship from Alexandria, the port of Egypt, the breadbasket of the Roman Empire. There are 276 people on board—crew, passengers, soldiers, and prisoners, including three men of God.

This was not a cruise line love boat by any means. The voyage was strictly business, not pleasure. The season for sailing on the Mediterranean was really over. Acts 27:9 identifies the time as the days following the fast—Yom Kippur, the Day of Atonement—which would mean late September or early October. Sailing on the Mediterranean was risky in the fall and impossible in the winter. Paul's warning was dismissed by the ship's captain (v. 11), who elected to leave Fair Havens for Crete's better port of Phoenix for the winter. After all, down time was lost time, and the more progress they made toward Rome, the closer they were to payment for their journey. Surely the captain of the ship knew better than the feisty preacher in chains.

As they sailed westward, the skies turned black, the winds howled, and the seas boiled as a hurricane swept down upon them. With sails down, the ship was driven by the fierce winds, out of control. Every emergency measure possible was taken. Ropes were secured around the hull of the ship to strengthen it against the pounding of the seas and perhaps to reinforce it against the swelling pressure of the sea-soaked grain. As the storm grew more violent, the panic increased.

First, it was cargo that went overboard, then the ship's tackle. After days of raging seas, hope itself went overboard (v. 20). For two long weeks the storm hammered. They could not sleep; they did not eat. Everybody knew it was over. They would never make it.

This was Paul's situation. But change the calendar, the conditions, and the circumstances, and it can be any man's situation. Soft southern breezes don't last forever. The winds of life howl, the sun of life hides itself in darkness, and hope is gone.

Discouragement can come in the form of illness or in the loss of a job. It can show up as the death of a loved one or the death of a relationship. It can be trouble in the family or trouble in the church. It can be anything that takes from our hands the controls of our lives, so that we find ourselves on that razor's edge of pending disaster.

The psalmist, who knew some great moments of incredible accomplishments, also knew the dark night of the soul. He wrote:

> Save me, O God,
> > for the waters have come up to my neck
> > I sink in the miry depths,
> > where there is no foothold.
> I have come into deep waters;
> > the floods engulf me.
> I am worn out calling for help;
> > my throat is parched.
> My eyes fail,
> > looking for my God *(Ps. 69:1-3)*.

This is the way it was for Paul and his companions. Fourteen days of panic had drained all hope away. Thankfully, life is not always like that. But truthfully, life is often like that. In any group of people, behind the smile and the surface greetings, there is likely some battle of private desperation going on, a grim voice that shouts, "It's over. You'll never make it." In such an hour as this, God wants to get a word in to His people.

II. GOD'S ENCOURAGING PROMISE

The lowly preacher-prisoner had something to say to that beleaguered company of weary people. He clutched the rail of the storm-tossed ship and reminded them all, captain and centurion alike, that he had urged them not to leave the last port. A little holy "I told you so" seemed only natural in such a moment. But Paul had something far more significant to share, an incredible declaration that God had talked with him in the dark hours of the stormy night. Above the roar of the winds and the waves, the old preacher shouted good news: "I urge you to keep up your courage, because not one of you will be lost; only the ship will be destroyed. Last night an angel of the God whose I am and whom I serve stood beside me and said, 'Do not be afraid, Paul. You must stand trial before Caesar; and God has graciously given you the lives of all who sail with you.' So, keep up your courage, men, for I have faith in God that it will happen just as he told me. Nevertheless, we must run aground on some island" (vv. 22-26).

That is the way it was. In an unrelenting storm, in a hopeless situation, in a night without stars or rest—then and there, when life was falling apart, God came and said, "I am here. I have a plan for you. You can make it."

Here is the truth. God enters profoundly in the crisis. He comes with his grand word of peace, not in the great hours of success and accomplishment, but in the broken hours of our weakness. It's strange, isn't it?—the one thing we don't want is to be helpless, but it is in our helplessness that we are most open to God, and we find Him most available to us. Wisely did the hymn writer Sarah F. Adams write, "So by my woes to be / Nearer, my God, to Thee." This is not always the way it is, but it is frequently the case.

God got to Jacob when he was on the run for his life. When the pressure was off, Jacob seemed to forget all about God until once again his life was in jeopardy. But, behold—once again God is there, speaking and ready to do business (Gen. 28 and 32).

Moses knew the good life in Egypt—palatial surroundings and royal opportunities. But it was not until all of this was lost and he had passed his best years on the far edge of a barren desert that God really had an audience with him.

Isaiah was not yet all that God wanted him to be until King Uzziah was dead and the nation was in crisis. It was then that he heard God speak and found God's will.

John Wesley had high hopes and holy ambitions and all kinds of great dreams that collapsed in the real world of human effort. But through these failures God spoke and came.

Phineas F. Bresee was a successful Methodist minister who enjoyed the good life of well-to-do friends, corporate involvement, and tempting secular investments. But when an explosion in Mexico destroyed the silver mine and all his investment, Bresee found himself in both financial ruin and spiritual shadows. He had to uproot his family in 1883 by moving them from Iowa to California in a railroad freight car. Out of his embarrassment he made a new resolve never again to attempt to make additional money but to give himself to the direct preaching of the gospel.[1] When Bresee came to the end of himself, God was there saying, "You can make it, and I will help you."

God has significant matters with which He wants to confront us. He wants our attention, though too often He doesn't get it until the bottom drops out.

If you are in this place right now, get ready. This may be the very moment when you will hear God's Word to you. That's what happened to Paul. In that foreboding setting God spoke with a promise of his presence and a rebirth of hope. It was not just for Paul alone, but for all the 275 people with him. They dared to believe that the preacher was honest, that God could be trusted and there was no other way. God spoke—"You can make it. I am with you."

Fourteen days into the nightmare of the hurricane, the churning waters became shallow. At daybreak everyone on board shared their first meal in two weeks, with Paul, the prisoner, saying the blessing. Then it was on through the boiling surf and the shores of Malta, 276 soaked but safe people, 500 miles west of where they had last touched land. God said, "You can make it," and they did.

God said, "I am not finished," and He wasn't.

III. LIFE'S ENDURING PRINCIPLES

That was then; this is now. How does this apply to the present time and in our personal lives? We must be honest; ships at sea do not always make it to land. Wishing does not always make it so. There are relationships still broken and diseases that remain unhealed. There are dreams that seem to die before they have a chance.

There are also principles God uses to help turn darkness into day and to put life back together. Four of these principles are present in these verses.

The Principle of Commitment

The assurance of the words "You can make it" is based on the principle of *commitment*. Paul referred to "God whose I am" (v. 23). Commitment to the Lord God is always right, no matter what the outcome may be.

The greatest victory in life is to belong to Jesus Christ; to remain in Him is the grand accomplishment. Knowing Christ is not some gimmick that leads to great feats; it is the great fulfillment. If Paul had drowned in the depths of the Mediterranean, verse 23 would still be true: "God whose I am."

It's little wonder, then, that when life seems to be falling apart, the first thing God speaks to us about is our commitment to Him. Other things matter, but very little, if this is not cared for.

Too often we seek God to get out of a crisis, a reaction that misses the issue. In a crisis we ought to seek God for *himself.* When that's done, whatever else happens will be OK. God's heart is joined to those of people like Joshua who say in rugged commitment, "As for me and my household, we will serve the LORD" (Josh. 24:15).

The Principle of Obedience

The assurance of the words "You can make it" is also based on the principle of *obedience*. Paul said, "God whose I am and whom I serve" (v. 23). There's no way to dissociate Christian commitment from Christian obedience. It's all a part of the gospel package. One of the devil's lies is that it's possible to believe like a saint and live like Satan. Commitment means obedience.

The Bible tells us Jesus is the "source of eternal salvation for all who obey him" (Heb. 5:9). For Paul's trip to Rome, the issue was already settled on how he would live and what he would do when he arrived. Crisis conversion that does not lead to Christian conduct is not conversion at all—just an emotional scheme of escape.

The Principle of Trust

The assurance of the words "You can make it" is based on yet another principle: *trust.* Paul said, "Men . . . I have faith in God" (v. 25). In the face of the wind and the sea and the storm, he dared to believe that God's word was true, though at the moment he could see no evidence of it.

This is what the writer of Hebrews defined as faith: "Faith is being sure of what we hope for and certain of what we do not see" (Heb. 11:1). It is what the heroes of faith were commended for. Trust means we put our full weight down upon the trustworthiness of God and His Word.

The Principle of Endurance

The assurance of the words "You can make it" is based on one more principle: *endurance.* We are not told on which night of the raging storm God spoke or how many more nights and days of ceaseless tossing Paul endured before the ship thudded aground on Malta. But whether it was one or many, Paul kept believing even when it appeared that nothing was different— nothing except that he had heard God speak, and that was sufficient. Not the leap into the churning surf, nor the venomous snake in the fire, nor the ordeal in Rome could ever change Paul's assurance that God had come and declared, when life was falling apart, "You can make it. I am with you."

God, through His Son Jesus Christ, has the lovely habit of saying the same words to us.

One of my Christian heroes is Charles Colson. In many ways the life and witness of Colson is unique. The glory of his radical conversion and the impact of his life on our world are so much like that of Augustine. His first book, *Born Again,* chronicles his fall from political power in the Watergate scandal of 1972-73. It is a source of Christian inspiration to read of the Christian witness of Colson's friend, Tom Phillips, and Colson's dramatic and life-changing journey to faith in Christ.

On the last pages of Colson's books are moments that are just as moving as his conversion. Along with other powerful members of United States President Richard Nixon's staff, he had been sentenced to prison. On January 8, 1975, fellow prisoners John Dean, Herb Kalmbach, and Jeb McGruder were released from prison—but not Colson. On January 20, 1975, the Virginia Supreme Court announced that Colson had been disbarred, meaning he could never practice law again. On January 22, 1975, he was summoned to a prison office to receive a phone call from his attorney telling him that his son, Chris, a college freshman, had been arrested on drug charges. This was a low point beyond description in Colson's life.

In the midst of that emotional darkness, Colson made a total surrender to God, completing what he had begun on that night of witness with Tom Phillips some 18 months before. With his commitment came the joy and peace of turning everything over to God. He found more strength than he had experienced.

Two days later the orders arrived for Colson's release from prison. While escorting him to the prison gate, the marshal shared that he had had the feeling that God would set Colson free that day.

Colson replied, "He did it two nights ago."[2]

"Trust Me"

2 Cor. 12:7-10

W. T. Purkiser had a long and distinguished career in the Lord's service. Through his work as professor, president of Pasadena College, and editor of the *Herald of Holiness,* he had a profound influence on many lives, including mine. Of his many books, the one that I most often give out to people is *When You Get to the End of Yourself.* It was written out of his own spiritual journey as he and his family wrestled, and finally came to terms, with that deadly enemy cancer, which claimed his 39-year-old daughter, Joyce, in what should have been her prime of life. This good man of God wrote:

> Life can be terribly hard for most people some of the time and for some people most of the time. There is no easy way to explain this. We cannot understand why the dark night of the soul should come. We probably should not pretend that we do. But come it does, and we must learn to live with it without bitterness or self-pity. It is not that God loves some more than others. Nor is it that untroubled times are evidence of His special favor. To suppose that unruffled seas and blue skies are a token of divine approval is the cruel conceit of those with whom all things go well. . . .

> When you get to the end of yourself, you step out—not into darkness and the void—but into the strong arms of God. When we cannot understand, we can trust. When we cannot see, we can walk by faith.[1]

When God speaks, what does He say? We have been discovering what He had to say to His special ambassador, Paul. And what Paul tells us is that in a situation of limiting affliction and seemingly unanswered prayer, God says, "Trust Me." It is the word He says to all His children somewhere on their journey toward heaven and home.

1. THE AFFLICTION OF PAUL

No one lives in a vacuum. Each of us is both a producer and a product of our particular situations. This was true of Paul.

The church at Corinth had been established on his second missionary journey. It was the place where God announced, "I have people on my heart" (see Acts 18:10). Paul stayed in Corinth for a year and a half, a ministry surpassed in length only by his time in Ephesus later on. With the help of Aquila and Priscilla, Paul planted the light of Jesus in the darkness of Corinth. God took raw pagans and made them over again, resulting in new people.

But Corinth was the place where the church struggled hard to become what it should be. No other fellowship in those beginning days was as tangled, no other church was as fractured, as the church at Corinth. They wrangled over leadership, ethics, and principles. The letters of Paul to Corinth are filled with problems to be solved, as well as doctrine to be believed.

The last four chapters of 2 Corinthians present a vindication of Paul's ministry to that congregation. There were those in Corinth who, for whatever reason, had little or no use for Paul. If he had been voted on as pastor, it's likely he would have been voted down.

Paul did not greatly care if people thought less or more of him than they did of Peter or Apollos, but he did care immensely if the church would be hurt by these attitudes. Therefore, he defended himself, not out of arrogance, but out of awareness that the truth must be fought for and the church be protected.

Paul reviewed his godly service, rendered at the costly price of personal sacrifice. Beginning with chapter 11, verse 23, he catalogs what carrying his cross for Christ had required:

Are they servants of Christ? (I am out of my mind to talk like this.) I am more. I have worked much harder, been in prison more frequently, been flogged more severely, and been exposed to death again and again. Five times I received from the Jews the forty lashes minus one. Three times I was beaten with rods, once I was stoned, three times I was shipwrecked, I spent a night and a day in the open sea, I have been constantly on the move. I have been in danger from rivers, in danger from bandits, in danger from my own countrymen, in danger from Gentiles; in danger in the city, in danger in the country, in danger at sea; and in danger from false brothers. I have labored and toiled and have often gone without sleep; I have known hunger and thirst and have often gone without food; I have been cold and naked. Besides everything else, I face daily the pressure of my concern for all the churches. Who is weak, and I do not feel weak? Who is led into sin, and I do not inwardly burn? *(2 Cor. 11:23-29).*

To read such a record of the cost of serving Christ is to ask oneself, "What has it cost me to follow Jesus? Where is the cross in my discipleship?"

The point is not to prove to others that I am somebody but to remind myself that I am His.

In chapter 12, verses 1-4, Paul changes his focus and shares an intimate moment of his personal testimony. While his conversion has been the repeated core of his witness, he here discloses a time in his life, some 14 years earlier, when he was lifted into the very presence of God. Nowhere else does he mention this holy ground, and even here he parts the curtain only slightly. The event was so mystical and powerful that only the words of being "caught up to the third heaven" (v. 2) could begin its description. Still, Paul says, "I will not boast about myself, except about my weaknesses" (12:5).

Truly great men are humble. Truly godly men are even more so. The world says, "If you did it, you're not bragging." But there is a caution in the Spirit-filled life that counsels, "May I never boast except in the cross of our Lord Jesus Christ" (Gal. 6:14).

And then, along with this impressive record of sacrifice and service, joined with this testimony of mystical communion, Paul opens his heart in honest confession of personal suffering.

"To keep me from becoming conceited because of these surpassingly great revelations, there was given me a thorn in my flesh, a messenger of Satan, to torment me. Three times I pleaded with the Lord to take it away from me" (2 Cor. 12:7-8). *The Living Bible* expands upon this "thorn in my flesh" as "a messenger from Satan to hurt and bother me, and prick my pride."

What exactly was that thorn in the flesh that drove the great preacher to his knees time and time again? No one knows for sure. Some say it was epilepsy, or possibly even migraine headaches. Some think the reference in Gal. 6:11 to his writing in large letters is a suggestion of eye trouble. But no one knows for sure. Therefore, all of us can identify with him about any problem in our situation that does not go away and continues to keep us off balance, frustrated, defeated, and hurting. Whatever the thorn, it is what everyone wants to avoid and life says that no one avoids—not even the people of God who walk closely, work diligently, and sacrifice greatly.

II. The Answer of God

Think first of what God did not do. He did not take away the thorn, the affliction that Paul, so mighty in spirit and service, in prayer and power asked Him to remove. To that prayer God said No, for reasons we do not fully understand.

On the eve of His death, Jesus prayed for the cup of the Cross to be taken away from Him if possible (Matt. 26:39, 42). It was not possible, and it was not taken away.

God answers prayer in one of four ways: "No," "Slow," "Grow," or "Go." We prefer the "Go," the "Yes" of God to our prayers, because His yes signals our help, deliverance, achievement, and healing.

But the no of God may be as much a sign of His power and goodness as His yes may be. Dr. Purkiser wrote, "Soft nests are for little birds, and whatever God wants His people to be, it is not that they be little."[2]

God did not take away the thorn, and furthermore, as best we can know, God never did fully explain why He did not. It is doubtful that any of us will ever fully understand the why of our deepest disappointments. Most likely, we will suffer as did Job, who never found out why he suffered, not even when his suffering turned again into sunshine.

God says, "Trust Me." "My grace is sufficient for you, for my power is made perfect in weakness" (v. 9). Here is a deep lesson of the heart of faith: all the limitations, all our infirmities, all the disappointments of our failures, all the pains of our journey, just as much as our blessings and maybe more so—may have a place in God's good plan to make us His and to make us holy and more like Jesus.

Some unknown but wise and humbled soul wrote:
Not till the loom is silent and the shuttles cease to fly
Will God unroll the canvas and explain the reason why.
All the dark threads are as needful in the Master's skillful
*   hands,*
As the threads of gold and scarlet in the pattern He has
*   planned.*

It is not that the thorns of life are blessings in and of themselves. They are not. They hurt and infect and rob and destroy. But as they bring us to the Lord, they perform a blessed ministry, driving us to the only fountain where the Water of Life is truly found.

Wherever it may be that life has hurt you—relationships, health, family, possessions, profession—God says, "Trust Me. My grace really is sufficient for you."

III. THE ACCEPTANCE OF GRACE

Here, then, is Paul's blessed disposition of the matter: "I will boast all the more gladly about my weaknesses, so that Christ's power may rest upon me. That is why, for Christ's sake, I delight in weaknesses, in insults, in hardships, in persecutions, in difficulties. For when I am weak, then I am strong" (12:9-10).

We are not told how long it took Paul to reach this point of trust. It seems that it was his clear response of faith to the surprising announcement of God. In so many ways, this prayer of submission is the highest, most powerful form of prayer. One may describe prayer as composed of many elements. I see six such strands.

Prayer is *praise,* honoring and worshiping God for who He

is. Prayer is *thanksgiving,* giving gratitude to God for His blessings and care. Prayer is *petition,* asking God fervently for the
needs of our lives. Prayer is *intercession,* coming to God on be-
half of others and their needs of every kind. Prayer is *confession,*
laying before God with repentant heart the sins and failures of
our doing. Prayer is *surrender,* giving the whole matter over to
God and letting Him decide what is best and accepting what He
decrees.

For most of us, prayer is played out only on the string of
petition, "Give me, give me, give me." And petition certainly has
its place, both biblically and emotionally. So Paul urged the
Philippian church, "Do not be anxious about anything, but in
everything, by prayer and petition, with thanksgiving, present
your requests to God" (Phil. 4:6). But to the Ephesians he wrote,
"Pray in the Spirit on all occasions with all kinds of prayers and
requests" (Eph. 6:18).

That has to bring us sooner or later to the prayer of surrender—"Not as I will, but as you will" (Matt. 26:39). Indeed, this is
the most profound and most powerful of all prayers. It is not
quitting but rather yielding to God. It is not giving up but giving
over to the Lord. Surrender declares, "I will not doubt, but I will
trust God," and in so doing finds the poise and strength that en-
ables us to stand and proceed.

God says, "Trust Me."

Paul says, "I will," and in so doing he discovers strength
from God that would never have been his if the thorn had been
removed.

God still comes to each of us, His children, with the same
message, in the midst of our thorns of whatever definition, saying, "Trust Me."

There are so many things in life that we cannot explain or
understand. We don't really know why bad things happen to
good people. We really can't understand why life is so often
more difficult and disappointing than we think it should be. We
are forced to pour out our "Why?" to God. If we are to find reso-
lution to the matters, we, too, like Paul, must come to the altar
of surrender and, to the God who says, "Trust Me," cry out, "I
will."

If I understand this passage correctly, God says to the "whys?" of our lives three things.

First, God says, "This thing you do not want can be the thing that brings you to Me if you will trust Me." That, we would agree, is not bad but good.

Francis Thompson in his epic poem "The Hound of Heaven" has God saying that He does not take things from us for our harm but only that we might find it in His arms.

Second, God says, "This thing you do not want can be the thing that moves you to make Me Lord of all." Somewhere we must pray the prayer of surrender if we are to live the life of full surrender. Only as we are fully His without reservation can He be fully ours without limitation.

George Matheson walked the lonely road of surrender and made the discovery of sufficient grace. Stricken with blindness at the beginning of his ministry, this great soul of the 19th century wrote in words that still call hungering souls to live deeper in Christ.

> *Make me a captive, Lord,*
> *And then I shall be free;*
> *Force me to render up my sword,*
> *And I shall conqueror be.*

> *I sink in life's alarms*
> *When by myself I stand;*
> *Imprison me within Thine arms,*
> *And strong shall be my hand.*

Third, God says, "The thing you do not want, if yielded to Me, can be the thing that prepares you and equips you to minister to others." Those who help us most are those who understand, who have fought the same battles, struggled with the same disappointments, but have found their strength at the place of surrender. In turn they become light for our darkness.

A seminary classmate and college professor said to me, "My life has been a journey over the ashes of my broken dreams." Perhaps that's why God has been able to use the humility of his godly life as such an enduring source of encouragement to young people seeking to make both sense and progress in their own walk with God.

When God speaks, what does He say? Paul tells us that God said to him, "Trust Me." At some point on our walk with Him, that will be His word to us. That commitment of surrender will be our greatest source and discovery of strength.

Said one great soul of God, "Where faith is, no answer is needed. Where faith is not, no answer will suffice."

The late Bob Benson's wife, Peggy Benson, shared with me that a few days before Bob died of cancer, she was standing behind him as he washed his hands and face at the basin in his hospital room. As she supported his weakened body, her eyes met his eyes in the mirror. She asked him, "Did you talk with God today?"

Bob said, "Yep."

"Did you ask Him why He's letting this happen to us?"

"Yes."

"What did God say?"

"He said, 'When you get to the place that you know the answer, the question won't matter anymore.'"

Trust leaves the matter with God and goes on with confidence.

Notes

Chapter 1

1. Nancy Gibbs and Richard Ostling, "God's Billy Pulpit," *Time,* November 15, 1993, 74.

2. Mark Kreidler, "One of a Kind," *Sacramento Bee,* September 7, 1995, A-1.

3. Ibid., 12.

4. Bob Benson, *See You at the House* (Nashville: Generoux, 1986), 204. Used by permission of Peggy Benson, 3404 Richards St., Nashville, TN 37215.

Chapter 2

1. Albert Edward Day, *Existence Under God* (New York: Abingdon Press, 1958), 82.

2. C. S. Lewis, *The Problem of Pain* (New York: Macmillan, 1962), 93.

3. Dallas Mucci, *This Pair of Hands: Howard Hamlin, M.D., Man with a Mission* (Kansas City: Beacon Hill Press of Kansas City, 1988), 96.

Chapter 3

1. Glenn Daniels, *The Inspiring Life and Thoughts of Billy Graham* (New York: Paperback Library, 1961), 35. Also Gibbs and Ostling, "God's Billy Pulpit," 74.

2. Hoyt Stone, *Moments* (Kansas City: Beacon Hill Press of Kansas City, 1975), 33.

Chapter 4

1. Billy Graham, *World Aflame* (New York: Pocket Books, 1965), 182.

2. Wendy Murray Zoba, "Bill Bright's Wonderful Plan for the World," *Christianity Today,* July 14, 1997, 14.

3. John Bunyan, *The Pilgrim's Progress* (New York: Washington Square Press, 1961), 11.

Chapter 5

1. Timothy Smith, *Called unto Holiness: The Story of the Nazarenes. The Formative Years* (Kansas City: Nazarene Publishing House, 1962), 95.

2. Charles Colson, *Born Again* (Old Tappan, N.J.: Chosen Books, 1976), 340.

Chapter 6

1. W. T. Purkiser, *When You Get to the End of Yourself* (Kansas City: Beacon Hill Press of Kansas City, 1970), 11.